UNREST ON THE GOLDFIELDS

THE EUREKA REBELLION

Carmel Reilly

Unrest on the Goldfields: The Eureka Rebellion

Text: Carmel Reilly
Publishers: Tania Mazzeo and Eliza Webb
Series consultant: Amanda Sutera
Hands on Heads Consulting
Editors: Jarrah Moore and Sarah Layton
Project editor: Annabel Smith
Designer: Leigh Ashforth
Project designer: Danielle Maccarone
Permissions researcher: Lumina Datamatics
Production controller: Renee Tome

Acknowledgements
We would like to thank the following for permission to reproduce copyright material:

Front cover, p. 23 (top): Francis Farmar. All rights reserved 2024/Bridgeman Images; p. 4 (top): Ferres, John/STATE LIBRARY VICTORIA, (bottom): J. B. (John Black) Henderson/State Library of NSW; p. 5 (top): Chronicle/Alamy Stock Photo, (bottom): Visun Khankasem/Shutterstock.com; p. 6: Gill, S. T/STATE LIBRARY VICTORIA; p. 7 (top): Gill, S. T/STATE LIBRARY VICTORIA, (bottom): Chronicle/Alamy Stock Photo; p. 8 (top): Chronicle/Alamy Stock Photo, (bottom): ilbusca/DigitalVision Vectors/Getty Images; p. 9 (top) STATE LIBRARY VICTORIA, (middle): Paul A. Straub, (bottom right): Yaroslaff/Shutterstock.com, (bottom left): 169169/Adobe Stock Photos; p. 10: Philip Game/Alamy Stock Photo; p. 11: Walker Art Library/Alamy Stock Photo; p. 13: iStock.com/duncan1890; p. 14 (top): State Library Victoria, (bottom): Chronicle/Alamy Stock Photo; p. 15: Vintage Archive/Alamy Stock Photo; p. 16 (top): The Picture Art Collection/Alamy Stock Photo, (bottom): Public Record Office Victoria; p. 17: Darling Archive/Alamy Stock Photo; p. 18 (top): iStock.com/Whitehavengirl, (bottom): Becker, Ludwig. (1856). Peter Lalor Retrieved August 12, 2024, from http://nla.gov.au/nla.obj-137404456; p. 19: Gill, S. T. (1869). The license inspected/S.T.G./ State Library Victoria; pp. 1, 20: Lakeview Images/Alamy Stock Photo; p. 21 (bottom): daniiD/Shutterstock.com; p. 22: D and S Photography Archives/Alamy Stock Photo; p. 23 (bottom): Victorian Collections; p. 24: Pictorial Press Ltd/Alamy Stock Photo; p. 25: Museums Victoria, (bottom): Theodore King, The First Parliamentary Election, Bendigo, 1855, 1855. Collection Bendigo Art Gallery, Gift of Mr. J.S. Dethridge, 1894. Photograph by Ian Hill; p. 26 (top): Ballarat Heritage Services/Victorian Collections, (bottom): David Syme and Co. 1887/State Library Victoria; p. 27 (top): Becker, Ludwig. (1856). Peter Lalor Retrieved August 12, 2024, from http://nla.gov.au/nla.obj-137404456, (bottom): 19th era/Alamy Stock Photo; p. 30: Ham, T., & Tulloch, D. (David). (1851). Great Meeting of Gold Diggers Dec15th 1851 [picture] /engraved by Thomas Ham; drawn by D. Tulloch; p. 32: Roman Bodnarchuk/Adobe Stock Photos; back cover, p. 21 (top): Andrew Atkinson/DreamsTime.com.

Every effort has been made to trace and acknowledge copyright. However, if any infringement has occurred, the publishers tender their apologies and invite the copyright holders to contact them.

NovaStar

ISBN 978 0 17 033486 0

Cengage Learning Australia
Level 5, 80 Dorcas Street
Southbank VIC 3006 Australia
Phone: 1300 790 853
Email: aust.nelsonprimary@cengage.com

For learning solutions, visit **cengage.com.au**

Printed in China by 1010 Printing International Ltd
1 2 3 4 5 6 7 29 28 27 26 25

Nelson acknowledges the Traditional Owners and Custodians of the lands of all First Nations Peoples. We pay respect to Elders past and present, and extend that respect to all First Nations Peoples today.

CONTENTS

THE EUREKA REBELLION

The Eureka **Rebellion** was a series of **defiant** acts by gold miners during the Victorian gold rush in Australia in the 1850s. It is considered a very important event in the history of modern Australia.

The rebellion began in 1851, after the government of the **colony** of Victoria made a law that said miners on the goldfields had to pay a fee to receive a gold **licence**. Without a licence, they weren't allowed to mine for gold in Victoria. The miners felt the fee was unfair. They were also unhappy about their treatment by police on the goldfields, and the fact that they could not vote in the colony's **elections**.

a gold licence

After years of protests and conflicts, the rebellion came to an end in 1854, when the miners were defeated by soldiers in a battle at the Eureka Stockade in Ballarat.

Miners fight soldiers from behind a barricade at the Eureka Stockade.

THE EUREKA STOCKADE

The Eureka Stockade was a wooden **fortress** that was built by miners near the Eureka Mine to defend themselves against soldiers. The word "eureka" comes from ancient Greek and means "I have found it". People on the goldfields often shouted "Eureka!" when they discovered gold.

Miners discover gold and shout for joy.

Although the miners lost the battle at the Eureka Stockade, they won their fight for justice. Only a few months after the battle, the government admitted that the miners had been treated unfairly. The government dropped the gold licence fee and agreed to give miners the right to vote.

The miners' fight for fairness, freedom and equality helped to shape the nation of Australia and the government it has today.

Australia has become a fairer and freer nation because of the Eureka Rebellion.

THE GOLD RUSH

The gold rush in the colony of Victoria was one of many gold rushes around the world in the mid-nineteenth century. Gold was found around Ballarat and Bendigo in Victoria in 1851. News of its discovery spread quickly, and, within months, thousands of people had "rushed" into the area. Tent towns sprang up wherever gold was found.

In 1850, before the rush, there were about 70 000 people living in Victoria. By 1855, there were almost 320 000 – four times as many! By 1861, the gold rush had made Victoria into the largest and richest colony in Australia.

Miners lived in tent towns to be close to the goldfields.

GOLDFIELDS OF VICTORIA

Victorian gold rush towns grew bigger to fit their many new occupants.

"Panning" was one way to find gold by using water in a wide, shallow pan to separate gold from soil.

Life on the goldfields, or "diggings", as they were also known, was hard. Miners usually worked six days a week, from sunrise until sunset. Digging and panning for gold was back-breaking. Most miners lived in canvas tents. Diseases and accidents were common. Due to the harsh work and living conditions, miners often had bad health.

While some miners discovered enough gold to make them rich, most people who came to the diggings found very little. The wealthiest people were shopkeepers and hotel owners, who sold mining supplies, food and alcohol to the miners.

The goldfields were full of miners, but very few became wealthy.

THE 1851 GOLD LICENCE

Governor Charles La Trobe

As thousands of people rushed to Victoria for gold, the colony's **governor**, Charles La Trobe, began to worry. The colony had only been established in July 1851, just a few weeks before the gold rush began. It did not have **services** and things like good roads or a proper police force to meet the needs of all the new arrivals.

Governor La Trobe decided to introduce a law that said miners moving to the goldfields had to buy a gold licence. His idea was that the money made from selling licences would help pay for the new services. He also believed that the cost of a licence would discourage many people from coming to Victoria, which would help to keep the goldfields from becoming overcrowded.

The government set the cost of the licence at one and a half pounds (or one pound and ten shillings) per month. This was a lot of money at the time. Most families were earning around two or three pounds a month.

The cost of a gold licence was too much for most workers at the time.

In the 1800s, Melbourne (Victoria's biggest city) was a lot smaller than it is now, with fewer services.

MONEY IN THE COLONY

For most of the nineteenth century, Victoria, like all Australian colonies, used British pounds as currency, or money. One pound was made up of 20 shillings. One shilling was made up of 12 pence, or pennies.

£1 coin

shilling coins

penny coin

ANGER ON THE GOLDFIELDS

Governor La Trobe's gold licence law did not stop people from arriving at the goldfields. Thousands of them continued to flow into the colony every month. What's more, the governor soon realised the money from the licences was not enough to pay for the new services that were needed, either.

Miners soon began complaining about the cost of licences. One pound and ten shillings was too much for most people to pay, especially before they had even begun to pan or dig for gold.

They were also angry about the police, who had the power to arrest miners for not carrying a licence. The police regularly treated miners like criminals and could lock them up in **gaol** until they paid a large fine. Miners could be arrested even if they had simply left their licence in their tent! To make matters worse, the police often failed to protect people from crime on the goldfields.

The old Castlemaine Gaol was built in the gold rush and would have held miners.

Some miners also felt strongly about their lack of **democratic rights** in the colony. They believed the problems on the goldfields came from the fact that the government would not listen to them. Miners weren't allowed to vote in government elections, so they had no say in choosing their leaders and changing the laws that affected miners.

Miners began to hold meetings and organise small protests against the gold licence.

Tensions ran high among the miners themselves, but the new laws gave them a common interest.

DEMOCRACY

"Democracy" means "government by the people". The word comes from two Greek words: *demos*, meaning "people", and *kratos*, meaning "rule or power". Democracy is based on the ideas of freedom and fairness.

There are two kinds of democracy: direct democracy and **representative** democracy. In a direct democracy, people are able to have a direct say in the things that affect them. This works well for small groups. However, when there are large numbers of people, representative democracy works best. In a representative democracy, members of a large group vote in an election to choose a much smaller group of people to represent them, or act for them, in government. Once the representatives form a government, they then work together to run the country and make laws.

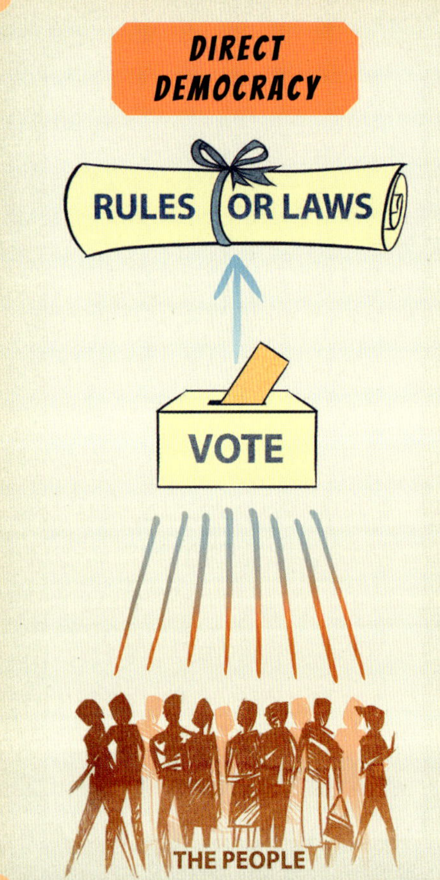

Representative democracies make sure all voices can be heard, and common interests can be found.

VOTING IN 1850s VICTORIA

In modern-day Australia, anyone who is a **citizen** and over the age of 18 has the right to vote. But in the early 1850s in Victoria, the only people who were able to vote were white men aged over 21 who owned land. This was less than 10 per cent of the population! What's more, half of the people in government were not voted in, but were instead given the job by the governor, who was the leader of the government.

Most miners, like other workers in the 1850s, didn't own land. Because of this, they could not vote or have their interests heard in parliament.

The Australasian Federal Convention drafted Australia's first constitution in 1891 – before this, each colony governed itself.

THE BUILD-UP TO REBELLION

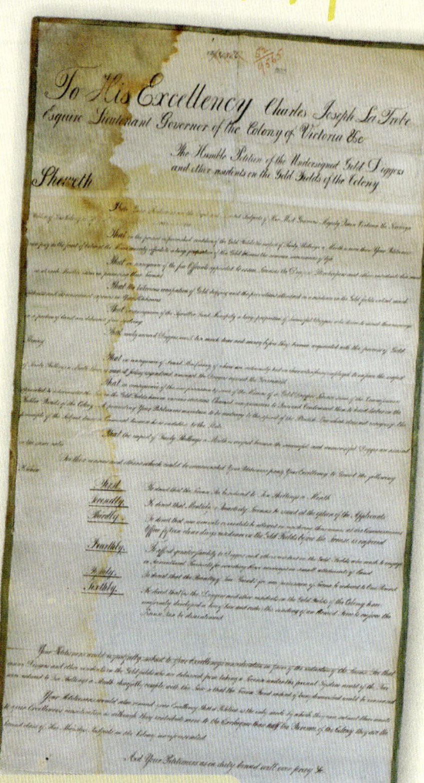

To His Excellency Charles Joseph La Trobe Esquire Lieutenant Governor of the Colony of Victoria &c

The Humble Petition of the Undersigned Gold Diggers and other residents on the Gold Fields of the Colony

Sheweth

the miners' petition, 1853

Despite the miners' anger about the gold licence fee, little changed over the next two years. If anything, conditions became worse as thousands more people arrived at the goldfields throughout 1852 and 1853. Miners continued to protest and hold meetings to voice their unhappiness.

In August 1853, thousands of miners in Bendigo signed a **petition** and sent it to the government. The petition stated that most miners were poor and could not afford the licence fee. The petition asked to have the licence fee lowered and for the licences to last longer than just one month.

Miners and their families are watched by a police officer in a camp outside of Bendigo, Victoria.

NOT ENOUGH CHANGE

In reply to these demands, the government made a new law in December 1853. Licence fees would be reduced to 1 pound per month, 2 pounds per three months, 4 pounds for six months and 8 pounds for 12 months. However, the fees were still too high for many miners – and the fines for not having a licence became higher, too. The government also did nothing to make the goldfields better or safer places to live and work. Nor would it let miners buy land, build a house or grow food on the goldfields, which made it hard for miners to stay in one place for long.

Miners could only live in temporary structures and weren't allowed to buy land in the areas where they were mining.

LICENCE HUNTS

Govenor Charles Hotham

In June 1854, Charles Hotham replaced Charles La Trobe as governor of the colony. Miners were hopeful that Governor Hotham would improve life on the goldfields. Instead, he ordered the police to make surprise licence inspections, or "hunts", twice a week, to increase the money coming in from fines. To reward the police, the government allowed police officers to keep some of the money from the fines for themselves. As a result, police gave miners even more fines, often unfairly.

The Victorian Police Force was created in 1853.

THE EUREKA HOTEL

In October 1854, another dramatic event occurred. William Bentley, the owner of the Eureka Hotel in Ballarat, was accused of killing a miner called James Scobie during a fight. However, when Bentley went to court for the **trial**, the judge found him not guilty. Many miners believed Bentley had given the judge money to make sure he did not go to prison.

Upset that the judge had let Bentley go and that there was no justice for the miner who had been killed, a group of miners burned down the Eureka Hotel. When some of them were arrested and locked up in gaol, other miners demanded their release.

The government became alarmed at what was happening. They sent hundreds of extra police and soldiers to the goldfields at Ballarat to help keep things peaceful. However, this only enraged the miners, who saw the soldiers as a threat to their safety.

Miners burn the Eureka Hotel in Ballarat in 1854.

THE BAKERY HILL MEETING

On 29 November 1854, the Ballarat Reform League held a huge meeting of about 12 000 miners at Bakery Hill in Ballarat. The **league** was a new group that had only recently formed. As well as an end to licences, the group wanted democratic rights for miners.

A miners' meeting notice calls miners to gather on Bakery Hill.

Unhappy with the arrival of soldiers on the diggings, the miners at the meeting declared their anger at the government. Many of them burned their gold licences as part of the protest. An energetic Irish-Australian man called Peter Lalor was voted in as the league's leader.

Peter Lalor

Despite their anger, most miners went back to working at the diggings the next day. However, knowing that many of them had burned their gold licences at Bakery Hill, the government sent soldiers and police into the goldfields on a licence hunt. They arrested hundreds of miners. Other miners rushed in to try to stop the arrests, and fights broke out.

A policeman checks a miner's licence at the diggings.

THE EUREKA STOCKADE

As the soldiers and police made their way through the diggings, large numbers of miners stopped work and headed to Bakery Hill again. A noisy meeting was held, and Peter Lalor called on the crowd to come together and fight against the soldiers. With the Eureka Flag behind him, he led the miners in declaring:

We swear by the Southern Cross
to stand truly by each other,
and fight to defend our rights and ***liberties****.*

The group then moved on to the Eureka Mine, which was about half an hour's walk away. There, a flagpole was constructed, and the Eureka Flag was raised.

Led by Peter Lalor, miners raised the Eureka Flag at Eureka Mine.

EUREKA FLAG

The Eureka flag shows the Southern Cross, which is a group of stars that can only be seen clearly in the skies of the Southern Hemisphere. No one knows who designed or made the flag. However, many people think these stars were chosen by its designer as a symbol of unity for miners, most of whom were new to Australia, to represent everyone coming together and fighting for their rights.

BUILDING THE STOCKADE

Over the next three days, hundreds of miners prepared for battle by making a fortress at the Eureka Mine. This fortress became known as the Eureka Stockade. The miners built the stockade from whatever they could find. This included pieces of wood from mining equipment and overturned carts. Since the stockade was later destroyed, no one really knows what it looked like. But it was probably at least the size of two basketball courts – large enough to hold several hundred people inside it.

A stockade is a line or wall of strong wooden posts built to defend a place.

A SURPRISE ATTACK

By Saturday 2 December, the stockade was finished. No one thought that fighting would break out soon, because the next day was Sunday, which was a day of rest on the goldfields.

Feeling safe, many of the miners left the stockade and went to their tents to eat and sleep.

Most miners returned to their tents on Saturday, ready to rest on Sunday.

A group of almost 300 soldiers and police attacked the stockade early on Sunday morning. About 150 miners were inside, and many of them were asleep. What's more, the soldiers had guns and most of the miners did not. After about 15 minutes of fighting, the battle was over. By then, 22 miners (including one woman) and 5 soldiers had died. The police arrested 113 people.

Soldiers attack the Eureka Stockade early on Sunday morning, 3 December 1854.

During the fighting, Peter Lalor was shot in the arm and badly injured. However, he managed to escape and hide with friends in the town of Geelong. A large reward was offered by the government for his arrest, but the reward was never claimed. Most people sided with the miners and agreed with their complaints, and no one ever told the police where Lalor was. He came out of hiding a few months later, when the reward for him was withdrawn.

V. R.

£400 REWARD

Whereas Two Persons of the Names of

Lawlor & Black,

LATE OF BALLAARAT,

Did on or about the 13th day of November last, at that place, use certain TREASONABLE AND SEDITIOUS LANGUAGE, And incite Men to take up Arms, with a view to make war against Our Sovereign Lady the QUEEN:

NOTICE IS HEREBY GIVEN

That a Reward of £200 will be paid to any person or persons giving such information as may lead to the Apprehension of either of the abovenamed parties.

DESCRIPTIONS.

LAWLOR.—Height 5 ft. 11 in., age 35, hair dark brown, whiskers dark brown and shaved under the chin, no moustache, long face, rather good looking, and is a well made man.
BLACK.—Height over 6 feet, straight figure, slight build, bright red hair worn in general rather long and brushed backwards, red and large whiskers, meeting under the chin, blue eyes, large thin nose, ruddy complexion, and rather small mouth.

By His Excellency's Command,

WILLIAM C. HAINES.

Peter Lalor's name was spelt incorrectly on the poster offering a reward for his arrest.

AFTER THE STOCKADE

Two important events took place as a result of the battle at the Eureka Stockade. The first was the forming of the Goldfields **Commission** of Enquiry. This was made up of a special group of people who were asked by the government to investigate life on the goldfields and consider the miners' claims. The second was the trials of 13 miners from the Eureka Stockade for high treason, or acting against the colony and the government.

THE GOLDFIELDS COMMISSION

In January 1855, the Goldfields Commission of Enquiry made a statement. It found that the goldfields had been badly run by the government. The Commission advised that the mining licence should be cancelled. It added that anyone in hiding since the Eureka Stockade should be given amnesty, meaning they should be forgiven for their actions. The Commission also suggested that miners should be given the right to vote in Victoria.

The miners' actions brought attention to their situation on the goldfields.

THE MINER'S RIGHT

A few months later, the government replaced the gold licence with a "miner's right", which cost one pound a year. As well as giving miners the right to mine gold, it allowed them to vote in the colony of Victoria, and to a buy a small piece of land and have a house and garden.

COLONY OF VICTORIA.

No 81 £1

DISTRICT Jamieson DATE 16 January 1865

Miner's Right.

ISSUED to Ralph Hogarth under the provisions of the Act of the Governor and Council, 21 Victoria, No. 32, to be in force until 15 January 18

NOT TRANSFERABLE.

A signed miner's right permitted a miner to dig for gold, vote and build a cottage and garden on a small area of land.

A gold miner painted this artwork of the first parliamentary election in Bendigo in 1855.

THE MINERS GO ON TRIAL

The 13 miners sit in court, on trial for high treason.

Throughout March 1855, each of the 13 miners charged with high treason faced a trial by **jury**. They were all found not guilty. Each of the juries was made up of local people, and almost all of them agreed with the miners' actions. The juries decided that the miners at the Eureka Stockade had not acted against the colony. Instead, the main aim of the miners was to improve life for people on the goldfields.

The freed miners were cheered by thousands of people in the streets of Melbourne.

VOTING RIGHTS AND A REPRESENTATIVE

In May 1855, the Victorian government made a new law that gave male miners the right to vote in Victoria. In 1857, this was extended to all men aged over 21, including First Nations men. Non-Indigenous women later won the right to vote in the state of Victoria in 1908.

In November 1855, Peter Lalor was voted in by the miners as their first representative in the Victorian government. He remained a government representative for over 20 years. He was known for always standing up for what he believed to be right and fair.

Peter Lalor as an older politician

Parliament House in Melbourne became the Victorian state government building, starting in 1856.

THE EUREKA REBELLION: A TIMELINE

1851 – 1 July: Victoria becomes an Australian colony with its own government.

21 August: Gold is discovered near Ballarat.

23 August: Governor La Trobe introduces the gold licence, which is a monthly mining licence fee of one pound and ten shillings.

1854 – June: Governor La Trobe is replaced by Governor Hotham.

September: Governor Hotham brings in twice-weekly gold licence "hunts".

October: Riots break out after William Bentley is found not guilty of killing a miner. The Eureka Hotel is burned down.

1 December: Miners start building a stockade.

3 December: Soldiers and police attack and defeat a group of miners at the Eureka Stockade.

1855 – January: The Goldfields Commission of Enquiry investigates the situation, and supports the miners' claims.

25 August

The first protest against the licence occurs.

1852

Protests continue.

1853

December

The cost of the gold licence is reduced, but fines are increased.

11 November

A group of miners form the Ballarat Reform League.

28 November

The government sends extra soldiers to Ballarat.

29 November

Gold licences are burned at a meeting of the Ballarat Reform League at Bakery Hill. The Eureka Flag is raised for the first time.

March

Miners who went to trial for high treason are found not guilty.

May

The gold licence is replaced by a miner's right, which also allows miners to vote in Victoria.

November

Miners vote in Peter Lalor as their first representative to government.

THE EUREKA REBELLION AND AUSTRALIAN DEMOCRACY

The Eureka Rebellion was about more than the cost of miners' gold licences. Miners realised that they were treated unfairly on the goldfields because they did not have any say in government or the right to vote. As the Ballarat Reform League declared, in its charter at Bakery Hill, it is the "right of every citizen to have a voice in making the laws he is called upon to obey".

For four years, miners at the Victorian goldfields stood together to create change. Many ideas based on equal opportunity and a "fair go" for all come from the Eureka Rebellion, and have helped to shape Australian democracy ever since.

The gold rush brought migrants from all over the world to Victoria, shaping the future of Victoria and Australia.

Glossary

citizen (*noun*)	a person who belongs to a country and has the same rights as everybody else there
colony (*noun*)	a country or area under the control of a more powerful country that is often far away
commission (*noun*)	a group of people who meet to organise or investigate something
defiant (*adjective*)	not obeying rules or orders
democratic rights (*noun*)	the rights to vote and be treated fairly by the government
elections (*noun*)	votes by the people to choose their leaders
fortress (*noun*)	a place that has been protected against attacks
gaol (*noun*)	a building where people were kept after they were arrested
governor (*noun*)	the official head of a colony or state
jury (*noun*)	a group of people at a trial who decide if a person is guilty of a crime
league (*noun*)	a group of people who come together for a particular purpose
liberties (*noun*)	freedoms and rights
licence (*noun*)	a certificate that allows somebody to do something, such as drive a car or dig for gold
petition (*noun*)	a letter signed by a large number of people asking those in power to do something
rebellion (*noun*)	when a group of people take action, or rebel, against their government
representative (*noun*)	a person chosen to act and speak for a group
services (*noun*)	systems to supply things people need, such as water, transport and medical care
trial (*noun*)	an official meeting to look at evidence and decide if somebody is guilty of a crime

Index